Messages of

ℒ𝒾𝑔𝒽𝓉

for **Advent** and **Christmas 2022**

Messages of

LIGHT

for **Advent** and **Christmas 2022**

3-MINUTE DEVOTIONS

MICHAEL WHITE and **TOM CORCORAN**

Ave Maria Press AVE Notre Dame, Indiana

Nihil Obstat:	Reverend Monsignor Michael Heintz, PhD
	Censor Librorum
Imprimatur:	Most Reverend Kevin C. Rhoades
	Bishop of Fort Wayne–South Bend
Given at:	Fort Wayne, Indiana, on 25 February 2022

Founded in 1865, Ave Maria Press is a ministry of the United States Province of Holy Cross.

www.avemariapress.com

Paperback: ISBN-13 978-1-64680-174-9

E-book: ISBN-13 978-1-64680-175-6

Cover and text design by Samantha Watson.

Printed and bound in the United States of America.

Introduction

The Advent and Christmas seasons offer many cherished traditions: watching Christmas movies, exchanging gifts, baking cookies. But one tradition is almost in a category by itself: Christmas lights.

Nothing quite feels like Christmas as much as Christmas lights. We adorn our homes, especially our Christmas trees, with them and seek out neighborhood displays of them. Some people take it even further: from the dazzling decorations of New York's Rockefeller Center to the festive and fun extravaganza on Thirty-Fourth Street right here in our hometown of Baltimore, blocks of homes and businesses are festooned in every conceivable way with lights. Since COVID-19 hit, we've even taken to decorating our campus here at Church of the Nativity with light displays to bring cheer into our community. It is already an established and beloved custom.

As the days are growing shorter and we experience so much darkness, we become more aware of our *need* for light. There is a universal hunger for light because light is life. Without light, nothing can live. Light is the very first link in the food chain. Our bodies crave light from the sun, a major source of the vitamin D we need to fight off infection and maintain good health. Then, of course, there is our need for light for our emotional health. Darkness depresses us, while light can lift our spirit.

Deeper than our physical and emotional needs for light is our souls' craving for it. Ultimately, whether we know it or not, that desire is for the light of Christ in our lives. We need his light to drive away the sin that is in our lives. Sin grows in the dark and hidden places of our soul. When Christ's light appears, it drives away all the ugliness and things we don't like about ourselves.

We must also look to the light of Christ to show us the way forward. When we don't know what to do or what is true, God wants to give us clarity and direction. Psalm 119:105 puts it best: "Your word is a lamp for my feet, a light for my path."

Once enlightened, we can come to realize that we too can be light for others; we can reflect the light of Christ for others. The apostle John wrote in his gospel, "All things came to be through him, and without him nothing came to be. What came to be through him was life, and this life was the light of the human race; the light shines in the darkness, and the darkness has not overcome it" (Jn 1:3–5).

In this season of the year, darkness seems to be winning. And at other times in our lives, darkness appears to have the upper hand too. But think about this: it only takes a little bit of light to fight back the darkness. And just a little bit of Christ's light can send the darkness fleeing. Only a few minutes of prayer each day can make a big difference in defeating the darkness around us. The light shines in the darkness, and the darkness has not overcome it.

We pray that these reflections will bring the light of Christ into your life and into the lives of your friends and family.

Fr. Michael and Tom
Church of the Nativity, Timonium, Maryland

First Week

OF ADVENT

Sunday, November 27

Christmas is the season of light. As we come into the darkest time of the year, we recognize more and more our need for light. In fact, light is life. We need light in every aspect of our beings.

We need it for our physical health. Without light, we have no food. Without light, we cannot manage our world and meet our needs.

We need light for our emotional health. Without light, we become depressed and sullen. Light brings a sense of confidence and security, while its absence can make us fearful and insecure.

We need light for our minds and hearts. Without the light of Christ in our minds and hearts, our minds are darkened with ignorance and our hearts are filled with fear. Over the next few weeks, we will look at our need for light and how to bear the light of Christ to others.

....

Ask Jesus to allow the light of his love into your mind and heart today.

Monday, November 28

In the beginning, when God created the heavens and the earth—and the earth was without form or shape, with darkness over the abyss and a mighty wind sweeping over the waters—

Then God said: Let there be light, and there was light. God saw that the light was good.

—Genesis 1:1–4a

Genesis tells us that in the beginning, the earth was without form or shape. In other words, it did not exist; there was nothing. There was nothing, and then God went to work to create the world. The first thing God created was light. Light is life.

Without light, we have no life. We have no food. We have no heat. We have no ability to move and meet our needs. Everything flows from the light that God created.

....

Thank God today for the light. Pray for the grace to live in God's light.

Tuesday, November 29

This is what Isaiah, son of Amoz, saw overcoming Judah and Jerusalem.

In days to come, The mountain of the LORD's house shall be established on the highest mountain and raised above the hills.

—Isaiah 2:1–2a

Isaiah spent time with God in prayer. As a result, Isaiah was able to see things others could not see, and God gave him a vision. In a period when people were turning away from God, Isaiah saw a time in which people will come to God's highest mountain. They will come to learn from God. In God's presence, Isaiah saw the light of a brighter future.

When we spend time with God in prayer, he can give us the light of his truth. God can shed light on the dark areas of our minds and hearts. Spending time with God allows us to see what we cannot possibly see on our own. This is why it is vitally important to pray every day. Prayer enlightens our minds and drives away the darkness of fear in our hearts.

....

Where do you feel in the dark right now? Share this with your heavenly Father. Ask him to allow his light into your mind and heart today.

Wednesday, November 30

All the nations shall stream toward it. Many peoples shall come and say: "Come, let us go up to the Lord's mountain, to the house of the God of Jacob, that he may instruct us in his ways, and we may walk in his paths." For from Zion shall go forth instruction, and the word of the Lord from Jerusalem.

He shall judge between the nations, and set terms for many peoples. They shall beat their swords into plowshares and their spears into pruning hooks; one nation shall not raise the sword against another, nor shall they train for war again.

—Isaiah 2:2–4

When people come to God, he brings peace. God imposes terms—meaning peace terms—and the people beat their swords into plowshares. Swords are used to wage war; plowshares are used to prepare dirt for sowing seeds. Spears are used to kill, but pruning hooks are small knives used to remove leaves and new shoots from grapevines to prune them for further growth.

Isaiah sees this great vision for the future. He sees people coming to God to learn his ways and encouraging others in his ways. He sees people coming to peace with one another.

....

Is there someone in your life whom you are fighting with right now? Do you need to put down your sword? Do you need to put down your spear? You have something that you are holding over them in your heart. Confess it to God and ask for the grace to make peace with them.

Thursday, December 1

He shall judge between the nations, and set terms for many peoples. They shall beat their swords into plowshares and their spears into pruning hooks; one nation shall not raise the sword against another, nor shall they train for war again. House of Jacob, come, let us walk in the light of the LORD!
—Isaiah 2:4–5

Isaiah sees a great vision in the future. He sees people coming to God to learn his ways. He sees people encouraging one another in God's direction. Peace comes as a result of everyone learning from God and encouraging each other in his direction. Isaiah, however, isn't just content with seeing this great vision; he sees it and then he calls people to action.

....

Let's not wait until the future; let's starting walking in God's light right now. We walk in God's light by learning from him in prayer and then putting into practice what we discover in prayer. Take a moment to read over the verses above. Ask God to help you prune away your pride and ego so you can live in peace with others instead of holding grudges in your heart.

Friday, December 2

He was in the beginning with God. All things came to be through him, and without him nothing came to be. What came to be through him was life, and this life was the light of the human race; the light shines in the darkness, and the darkness has not overcome it.

—John 1:2–5

John introduces his gospel by talking about Jesus as the light of the world. He is the true light of the world that is life. His light shines in the darkness, and the darkness has not overcome it. The darkness of evil could not overcome Jesus. His death meant not the end but instead the beginning of a new kind of life.

Light always defeats the darkness. As soon as a light is lit, the darkness flees. Even when darkness seems to be winning, it takes only a little bit of light to defeat it.

....

Where do you feel you are walking in darkness? Invite the light of Christ into your mind and heart.

Saturday, December 3

Psalm 147:1–2, 3–4, 5–6
Blessed are all who wait for the Lord.
Praise the LORD, for he is good;
    sing praise to our God, for he is gracious;
    it is fitting to praise him.
The LORD rebuilds Jerusalem;
    the dispersed of Israel he gathers.
Blessed are all who wait for the Lord.
He heals the brokenhearted
    and binds up their wounds.
He tells the number of the stars;
    he calls each by name.
Blessed are all who wait for the Lord.
Great is our LORD and mighty in power:
    to his wisdom there is no limit.
The LORD sustains the lowly;
    the wicked he casts to the ground.
Blessed are all who wait for the Lord.

Second Week

OF ADVENT

Sunday, December 4

As the days get darker and darker in this second week of Advent, we become more and more aware of our need for light. We need light for our physical and emotional health. We need the light of Christ for our spiritual and intellectual well-being.

Light is influential. When we are in a dark place or dark room, we naturally move toward the light because it gives us clear direction. The darker the place, the more we can be influenced by a light. Our lives are to be light for others so that we move in God's direction. No matter who you are, you can influence or be a light to other people. Influence is the power to affect how someone develops, acts, or feels. Influence moves people in one direction or another. God has put you on this earth to be a light that will influence people in his direction.

....

Ask God to help you grow this week to see how you can be a light for others. Pray for God to give you the names of people he wants you to move in his direction.

Monday, December 5

A man named John was sent from God. He came for testimony, to testify to the light, so that all may believe through him. He was not the light, but he came to testify to the light. The true light, which enlightens everyone, was coming into the world.
—John 1:6–9

The man to whom the gospel writer John refers is John the Baptist. John the Baptist had such a following and was so charismatic that many people came to believe he was the Messiah or the light God had sent into the world. But he wasn't the light. He pointed to Jesus, who is the light. John the Baptist came to bear witness to Jesus who is the true light so that everyone would believe in him. He came to prepare the way for Jesus.

As Christ followers, all of us are to be like John the Baptist. We are to bear witness and point the way to Jesus who is the true light of the world. We acknowledge that we have no light to shine on our own. The light and the good within us come because we live in a relationship with Jesus.

....

Take a moment to acknowledge Jesus as the light of the world and the light of your world.

Tuesday, December 6

In those days John the Baptist appeared, preaching in the desert of Judea [and] saying, "Repent, for the kingdom of heaven is at hand!"
—Matthew 3:1–2

John the Baptist first appeared in a unique place: the desert wilderness. There were few people in the desert, but he began preaching there anyway. There is great symbolism in this. It shows that the preaching in the Temple and synagogues was ineffective. God had to send someone outside of the religious establishment to prepare the way for his Son.

The austere place of the wilderness stood as a sign of John's radical service to God. He lived without any comforts. Throughout the scriptures, the wilderness is the place that God accomplishes his greatest work in people and prepares them to make a great impact.

In the desert, John the Baptist had a very specific message to help point people toward the light: "Repent, for the kingdom of heaven is at hand!" *Repent* means a change of thinking that leads to a change of heart that results in a change of action or direction. John challenges people to change their direction and turn back to God because he is near.

....

God has placed you in a specific location to bring his message to a certain group of people. Your life can be the light that helps someone change direction back toward God. Pray for God to give you the names of people he wants you to be a light for and move in his direction.

Wednesday, December 7

It was of him that the prophet Isaiah had spoken when he said: "A voice of one crying out in the desert, 'Prepare the way of the Lord, make straight his paths.'"

—Matthew 3:3

The prophet Isaiah had foretold that, before the Messiah came, someone would go out into the wilderness and prepare the way for him. At a certain point, John came to understand that this was to be his role in life. He must have been reading through the book of Isaiah and said, "That's it. That describes me. I am to be a light to others by living in the desert and telling people to prepare the way for the Messiah."

Each of us has a unique message to share with others. Our message comes out of our life experience as well as our interaction with the scriptures. There are certain passages of scripture that will resonate with you. Those messages are for you to communicate to others through your life.

....

Ask the Holy Spirit to remind you of the scripture passages or verses that resonate with you. (If you need help finding the passages, google the words or phrases you remember.) Ask God to show you how you can share those verses with others.

Thursday, December 8

John wore clothing made of camel's hair and had a leather belt around his waist. His food was locusts and wild honey.

—Matthew 3:4

John's message was communicated first by where he lived, then by what he said, and then by how he lived. John had a very simple and austere lifestyle. He wore uncomfortable clothes of camel's hair. He ate locusts and wild honey. That was it. He lived simply and austerely. His actions reinforced his message.

You do not have to live as John did to share the Gospel. There are some simple actions you can do to add value to people. They are actions that will enable you to point to the light of Christ.

Smile at people. When you smile at people, what happens? They smile back. When they smile back, that means you just influenced them. They did something they wouldn't have done because you made the choice to smile at them. Sometimes, it can turn their whole day around.

Call people by name. The sweetest sound to anyone is the sound of their own name.

Encourage others by noticing them doing good. Be on the lookout to encourage people in the smallest of accomplishments. Do small acts of service.

....

Ask the Holy Spirit to remind you to be a light to others today by adding value to their lives in small ways.

Friday, December 9

I am baptizing you with water for repentance, but the one who is coming after me is mightier than I. I am not worthy to carry his sandals. He will baptize with the holy Spirit and with fire.

—Matthew 3:11

Crowds of people left the city and went out into the middle of nowhere to hear John the Baptist preach and to be baptized by him. He used his popularity to direct people to Jesus. Where John lived, how he lived, and his message all worked together to point people to the light of Christ.

In the same way, everything in your life can point people to the light of Christ. It begins with where God has placed you. God has placed you wherever you are right now to be his light and to influence people in his direction. You may be stuck in a job that you don't like. You may be at a college you didn't plan to attend. You may live somewhere you don't prefer. But you are not where you are by accident. God has put you there to be a light and for a purpose.

God has shaped you uniquely to bring some people into a relationship with his Son. He has appointed you to be a light in this dark world that points people to the light of Jesus. That is not an obligation. It is not something you *have* to do. It is something you *get* to do.

....

Ask Jesus for the grace to be his light in our dark world. Thank him for the privilege of bringing others to him.

Saturday, December 10

Psalm 80:2ac and 3b, 15–16, 18–19

**Lord, make us turn to you; let us see your face
and we shall be saved.**

O shepherd of Israel, hearken,
From your throne upon the cherubim, shine forth.
Rouse your power.

**Lord, make us turn to you; let us see your face
and we shall be saved.**

Once again, O LORD of hosts,
    look down from heaven, and see;
Take care of this vine,
    and protect what your right hand has planted
    the son of man whom you yourself made
    strong.

**Lord, make us turn to you; let us see your face
and we shall be saved.**

May your help be with the man of your right hand,
    with the son of man whom you yourself made
    strong.
Then we will no more withdraw from you;
    give us new life, and we will call upon your
    name.

**Lord, make us turn to you; let us see your face
and we shall be saved.**

Third Week

OF ADVENT

Sunday, December 11

Jesus came into this world to save and redeem it through his whole life, death, and resurrection. His cross and resurrection are essential to this mission, but so are his life, teaching, and actions. The redemption of the world does not just mean Jesus came to save our souls from our sins. He came to bring about healing and redemption of the whole person and the whole of creation. His cures and miracles of healing were all signs of the greater work God was doing.

After Jesus died and rose from the dead, the early church continued his work. They knew him personally, and their mission was to bring about the redemption of the world by bringing people into a relationship with Jesus Christ. But they didn't just tell people about Jesus and preach about him. They acted as Jesus did. This is why the book describing their efforts is called the *Acts* of the Apostles. The apostles made an impact by caring for those whom no one else would care for. In a time when human life was cheap and disposable, they cared for people. They became a light in a very, very dark world.

....

Pray for our Church. Pray that we will work together to bring God's love and light into our dark world. Pray that our efforts will help people in need.

Monday, December 12

When John the Baptist heard in prison of the works of the Christ, he sent his disciples to him with this question, "Are you the one who is to come, or should we look for another?"

—Matthew 11:2–3

John the Baptist had an incredibly successful ministry. Still, he was humble and knew it wasn't about him. He was happy to point the crowds to Jesus and step out of the way because he was fully confident that Jesus was the Messiah. He enthusiastically embraced his role to prepare the way for Jesus.

That was before he was imprisoned. After spending a long time in prison, John the Baptist started to wonder whether it was all worth it. He assumed that if Jesus was truly the Messiah, he would have been freed from prison. The Messiah was supposed to make life better, yet his life wasn't better. Was Jesus really the Messiah, or should he hope for another?

When the world seems dark, we are more likely to doubt God's goodness and love. John feels this doubt. So he sends some of his followers, his disciples, to Jesus to ask if he is truly the Messiah or if they should look for someone else to fulfill that role.

....

If your life feels dark, ask Jesus if you should look for someone else. Share your doubts honestly with him and leave some space for him to speak to you.

Tuesday, December 13

When John the Baptist heard in prison of the works of the Christ, he sent his disciples to Jesus with this question, "Are you the one who is to come, or should we look for another?" Jesus said to them in reply, "Go and tell John what you hear and see: the blind regain their sight, the lame walk, lepers are cleansed, the deaf hear, the dead are raised, and the poor have good news proclaimed to them."
—Matthew 11:2–5

Jesus responds to John's request, but he doesn't speak of his great insights and teaching. He doesn't respond with theological language or argument. Jesus tells John's disciples to go and tell John what they see. He points to things that are visible, to concrete signs that he is the Messiah.

People were attracted to Jesus because he was a light in a dark world. They saw that he made people's lives better. They came to him and were healed. They came to him, and people who had previously been uncared for and thought of as unimportant received his love and attention. They mattered to him. The same is true for our lives. We are to be a light by proclaiming the good news of God's love through our care for the disadvantaged.

Who are the sick or disadvantaged God is calling you to care for? Ask the Holy Spirit to help you see the people he wants you to care for.

Wednesday, December 14

Strengthen the hands that are feeble, make firm the knees that are weak, say to the fearful of heart: Be strong, do not fear! Here is your God, he comes with vindication; with divine recompense he comes to save you. Then the eyes of the blind shall see, and the ears of the deaf be opened; then the lame shall leap like a stag, and the mute tongue sing for joy.

—Isaiah 35:3–6a

The prophet Isaiah predicted that when the Messiah came, good works would accompany him as a sign that he really is the Savior of the world. He would strengthen the hands of people who are faithful. The Savior strengthens hearts and tell us to fear not—because our God vindicates us, our God saves us. The Messiah opens the eyes of the blind and helps the deaf hear.

....

Jesus is the Messiah. He brings light into this dark world. He strengthens us and redeems us. Reflect on the verses above. Read them slowly. Ask Jesus to give you whatever you need. Pray that he will use you to be a light for others.

Thursday, December 15

Then Peter, filled with the holy Spirit, answered them, "Leaders of the people and elders: If we are being examined today about a good deed done to a cripple, namely, by what means he was saved, then all of you and all the people of Israel should know that it was in the name of Jesus Christ the Nazorean whom you crucified, whom God raised from the dead; in his name the man stands before you healed."

—Acts 4:8–10

The book of Acts tells us that Peter heals a crippled man. He uses this opportunity to preach about Jesus. The Jewish leaders arrest Peter and question him. Peter responds by noting that he is being questioned and punished for doing a good deed. Then he tells the elders that the man was healed in the name of Jesus. It was his power, his name, that gave Peter the power to do good.

As a Church and as Christ followers, we are to do the same. We are to bring healing and wholeness to others by the name and power of Jesus Christ. We are then to communicate that our good is done in his name and by his power.

....

Ask Jesus to use you today to bring his healing to a broken world. Ask for his power to heal others.

Friday, December 16

[Jesus said,] "You are the light of the world. A city set on a mountain cannot be hidden. Nor do they light a lamp and then put it under a bushel basket; it is set on a lampstand, where it gives light to all in the house. Just so, your light must shine before others, that they may see your good deeds and glorify your heavenly Father."

—Matthew 5:14–16

Jesus addresses this message to people living in Judea, in a backwater of the Roman Empire. The people in Judea did not feel as if they were the light of the world. They felt like nobodies. They felt put down by the ruling powers. Jesus gave them a new identity and a new purpose. He showed that their good deeds could shine before others and bring glory to God the Father.

Jesus speaks the same message to you. No matter who you are or what position you have, Jesus has positioned you to be a light in this dark world. That's an amazing privilege.

....

Pray for the grace to embrace your identity as a light for this dark world. Ask God to help you see the good deeds he wants you to do today.

Saturday, December 17

Psalm 72:1–2, 3–4ab, 7–8, 17

Justice shall flourish in his time, and the fullness of peace for ever.

O God, with your judgment endow the king,
    and with your justice, the king's son;
He shall govern your people with justice
    and your afflicted ones with judgment.

Justice shall flourish in his time, and the fullness of peace for ever.

The mountains shall yield peace for the people,
    and the hills justice.
He shall defend the afflicted among the people,
    save the children of the poor.

Justice shall flourish in his time, and the fullness of peace for ever.

Justice shall flower in his days,
    and profound peace, till the moon be no more.
May he rule from sea to sea,
    and from the River to the ends of the earth.

Justice shall flourish in his time, and the fullness of peace for ever.

May his name be blessed forever;
    as long as the sun his name shall remain.
In him shall all the tribes of the earth be blessed;
    all the nations shall proclaim his happiness.

Justice shall flourish in his time, and the fullness of peace for ever.

Fourth Week

OF ADVENT

Sunday, December 18

We are now in the fourth week of Advent, and we have continued to become more and more aware of our need for light. We need the light of Christ in our minds and in our hearts. We need the light of Christ to radiate from our lives. And we are called, challenged, and encouraged to bring the light of Christ to others.

As Christ followers, we are to let Christ's light into our lives. Yet, at times, our minds and hearts can be darkened by fear and doubt. Fear and doubt can tempt us to walk away from our responsibility to bring the light of Christ to others. We may fear rejection or what others might think. We may fear failure. We may doubt that God can use us to bring his light into the world.

....

Like us, Joseph had to overcome fear and doubt to bring Christ's light into the world. This week, we will learn from his story so that God can use us to bring the light of Jesus to others. Ask God to use you in these last few days before Christmas to bring the light of Christ to others. Pray that his grace will drive away all fear and doubt.

Monday, December 19

> Now this is how the birth of Jesus Christ came about. When his mother Mary was betrothed to Joseph, but before they lived together, she was found with child through the holy Spirit. Joseph her husband, since he was a righteous man, yet unwilling to expose her to shame, decided to divorce her quietly.
>
> —Matthew 1:18–19

In the culture Mary and Joseph lived in, couples would get engaged about a year before their actual marriage. Although legally married, a couple didn't live together or participate in the marital act. And yet, during this time, Mary became pregnant. Matthew is quick to point out that the child was conceived by a miracle, by the power of the Holy Spirit.

Matthew tells us that Joseph was a righteous man. He was a good and faithful servant of the Lord. He did God's will. While scripture does not tell us why Joseph planned to divorce Mary quietly, many scholars believe Joseph knew what was happening. He understood that a miracle had taken place but was filled with fear at the great task in front of him.

....

God gives us the great task of bringing his light to the world. Fear at fulfilling this task can overwhelm us. We might want to walk away from it. Confess any fears you have to God, and pray that he will lead you toward following his will.

Tuesday, December 20

Such was his intention when, behold, the angel of the Lord appeared to him in a dream and said, "Joseph, son of David, do not be afraid to take Mary your wife into your home. For it is through the holy Spirit that this child has been conceived in her. She will bear a son and you are to name him Jesus, because he will save his people from their sins."
—Matthew 1:20–21

Joseph intends to walk away from both Mary and the role God wants him to play. His mind and heart are filled with darkness and fear. Then God's angel appears to him. He tells Joseph not to be afraid, for it is by the power of the Holy Spirit that Mary has conceived the child. God is sending his Son into the world to save people from their sins. All of this is God's work. Joseph's role is simply to name God's Son.

God does all the heavy lifting in this world. God does the hard work. He invites our participation in what he is going to accomplish. We get to be part of his winning team, so we do not have to fear rejection from others or fear that he will not give us what we need. We do the possible, and God does the impossible.

....

Listen to God when he tells you not to be afraid. Pray for the grace to not let fear get in the way of bringing others to Christ and fulfilling the role God has for you.

Wednesday, December 21

> When Elizabeth heard Mary's greeting, the infant leaped in her womb, and Elizabeth, filled with the holy Spirit, cried out in a loud voice and said, "Most blessed are you among women, and blessed is the fruit of your womb. And how does this happen to me, that the mother of my Lord should come to me?"
>
> —Luke 1:41–43

Each individual who plays a role in the Christmas story participates by following the light of truth. God lights their way, and they respond with obedience. Elizabeth's role is to bless and affirm Mary in her role as the Mother of God. While Mary would have been criticized and looked down upon by many people in her hometown since she was pregnant yet not married, Elizabeth affirms her.

The Holy Spirit shows Elizabeth the truth about Mary—that Mary's child has been conceived by the power of God. Seeing Mary as God sees her, Elizabeth warmly welcomes Mary and encourages her.

....

In these days leading up to Christmas, ask the Holy Spirit to show you whom you can encourage and affirm. You may be asked to affirm someone who, in the world's eyes, does not have much value or whom you would normally criticize. Ask the Holy Spirit for his perspective on people so you can see what the world does not see.

Thursday, December 22

And Mary said: "My soul proclaims the greatness of the Lord; my spirit rejoices in God my savior. For he has looked upon his handmaid's lowliness; behold, from now on will all ages call me blessed. The Mighty One has done great things for me, and holy is his name. His mercy is from age to age to those who fear him."

—Luke 1:46–50

Mary visits her cousin Elizabeth after the angel Gabriel appears to her and she says yes to bringing God's Son into the world. Elizabeth encourages Mary, and then the Holy Spirit enlightens Mary. God has looked upon her humility with favor. Her yes to God means that all generations will bless her and revere her. God has done great things for her.

Our encouragement to others can help them see how God has blessed them. Our encouragement can be a light that helps others see the light of God's love for them. Our encouragement can light a way for people to see God's mercy at work in their lives.

....

Whom does God want you to encourage today? Ask the Holy Spirit to enlighten you. Pray for eyes to see and ears to hear.

Friday, December 23

When they came on the eighth day to circumcise the child, they were going to call him Zechariah after his father, but his mother said in reply, "No. He will be called John." But they answered her, "There is no one among your relatives who has this name." So they made signs, asking his father what he wished him to be called. He asked for a tablet and wrote, "John is his name," and all were amazed. Immediately, his mouth was opened, his tongue freed, and he spoke blessing God.

—Luke 1:59–64

Again we see how God enlightens everyone in the Christmas story to understand their role in salvation history. Joseph, Mary, and Elizabeth see their roles and embrace them instantly. Zechariah does not. He doubts the message of the angel Gabriel and, as a result, is struck dumb. He cannot speak until he agrees to name his child John as God commanded him. As soon as he opened his mouth he blessed and praised God.

We may not be struck dumb by refusing to live in the light of God's truth, but our refusal can keep us from bringing others to God. When we choose to live in darkness, our words no longer bring blessing to God and others. When we choose to accept God's light of truth into our lives, our words can bless God and bless others.

....

Pray for the grace today to accept the light of God's truth in your life. Agree with the truth of God's love in your life and pray for the grace to bless others today with your words.

Saturday, December 24

Psalm 89:2–3, 4–5, 27 and 29

For ever I will sing the goodness of the Lord.

The favors of the LORD I will sing forever;
>   through all generations my mouth shall pro-
>   claim your faithfulness.

For you have said, "My kindness is established
>   forever";
>   in heaven you have confirmed your faithfulness.

For ever I will sing the goodness of the Lord.

"I have made a covenant with my chosen one,
>   I have sworn to David my servant:

Forever will I confirm your posterity
>   and establish your throne for all generations."

For ever I will sing the goodness of the Lord.

"He shall say of me, 'You are my father,
>   my God, the rock, my savior.'

Forever I will maintain my kindness toward him,
>   and my covenant with him stands firm."

For ever I will sing the goodness of the Lord.

CHRISTMASTIME

Sunday, December 25

On this Christmas morning, we celebrate that Jesus is our Emmanuel. He is God with us. More than six hundred years before Jesus's birth, the prophet Isaiah had promised that he would send a savior into the world through a virgin. The Savior is God's very own Son. He is with us.

At every moment of every day, God is with us. This is the promise and blessing of Christmas. We never have to be alone because God has come to us. Christmas tells us that we do not have to strive to get to God because God has already come to us—in the humility of a little child.

....

Take this Christmas morning to reflect on the joy that God is with us.

Monday, December 26

All this took place to fulfill what the Lord had said through the prophet: "Behold the virgin shall be with child and bear a son, and they shall name him Emmanuel," which means "God is with us." When Joseph awoke, he did as the angel of the Lord commanded him and took his wife into his home. He had no relations with her until she bore a son, and he named him Jesus.

—Matthew 1:24–25

Joseph almost allows the darkness of fear to keep him from being an agent of light. The angel tells Joseph the larger story of which he is a part. He enlightens Joseph's mind and heart, explaining that he is part of God's great plan to save people from their sins. He makes clear Joseph's role to care for God's Son and the responsibility to name the child. Joseph does what he is called to do.

God wants to give us light in our minds and our hearts. He wants to give us the clarity of the truth in our minds. He wants to drive the darkness of doubt away. We must be open to the ways that God wants to speak to us. He speaks to each of us. To some people, he speaks through dreams. To others, he speaks through small signs. To everyone, he speaks through scripture and his Word. God brings the light, and we must be open to it and make ourselves available.

....

Take a moment to allow God to speak to you. Ask him to send his light into your mind and heart.

Tuesday, December 27

What was from the beginning, what we have heard, what we have seen with our eyes, what we have looked upon and touched with our hands concerns the Word of life—for the life was made visible; we have seen it and testify to it and proclaim to you the eternal life that was with the Father and was made visible to us—what we have seen and heard we proclaim now to you, so that you too may have fellowship with us; for our fellowship is with the Father and with his Son, Jesus Christ.

—1 John 1:1–3

The apostle John testifies that he has seen and touched the Son of God. He and others spent time with Jesus. They ate and hung out with Jesus. After spending time with him, they came to believe they were in the presence of the Son of God.

....

Jesus brings us the words of life and light. He wants to make visible and clear his presence and his direction for our lives. He wants to be as present to us as he was to the disciples. Where do you need Jesus's light and life in your life? Share it with him today. Ask him to have it made visible to you.

Wednesday, December 28

For all of you are children of the light and children of the day. We are not of the night or of darkness. . . . Therefore, encourage one another and build one another up, as indeed you do.
—1 Thessalonians 5:5, 11

As children of the light, we are aware of our need for light, especially the light of Christ. We need the light of Christ in our minds and in our hearts—and we are called, challenged, and encouraged to bring that light to others.

While we are to be light for others, we must return to prayer and scripture over and over again to receive Christ's light. As we travel through life, we hit times of darkness. We know how difficult it is to walk through life in the dark. The darkness in our lives can come in many different ways or by different names: an illness, unemployment, parenting, or marital issues. Darkness comes in many forms, and trying to navigate our way in the dark is not fun.

....

We are not of the dark, and God does not want us walking in the dark. He wants us to walk in the light, and he wants to be our light. As we prepare to walk into a new year, ask God to be your light.

Thursday, December 29

The people who walked in darkness have seen a great light; upon those who lived in a land of gloom a light has shown.

—Isaiah 9:1

Walking in the dark can be extremely unnerving. In the dark, we have to move more slowly and cautiously. We feel less comfortable and secure. Living our lives in the dark can feel gloomy as well. Our hearts and souls feel heavier and heavier when we are walking in the dark.

Isaiah describes the nation of Israel as walking in great darkness. They were in darkness because they had wandered away from God and his ways. Isaiah sees a day when the nation will see a great light. A light will dawn that will show them the way.

....

God wants to give us light for our dark times. His light will dawn. Our role is to be on the lookout for his light. Ask the Lord to show you his light in an area of your life that seems dark.

Friday, December 30

You have brought them abundant joy and great rejoicing; they rejoice before you as people rejoice at harvest, as they exult when dividing the spoils.
—Isaiah 9:2

There is an abundant joy when we see a way forward through the darkness of our problems toward a possible solution. It is a joy that rivals farmers celebrating at the harvest and rejoicing that they have so much food. We might think of the celebrations in the locker room or in a city after a team wins a championship after a long period of losses. It is pure joy when you begin to find a way forward out of the darkness of your problems.

God, your heavenly Father, wants you to have this kind of joy. Your heavenly Father does not want you to live in the darkness of fear. He doesn't want you living in the darkness of discouragement. Your heavenly Father does not want you to live in the darkness of confusion. He does not want you living in the darkness of shame or guilt. He wants you to experience the joy that comes from his light.

....

Thank your heavenly Father for wanting to give you joy from walking in his light. Thank him for being for you and not against you.

Saturday, December 31

Psalm 96:1–2, 11–12, 13
Let the heavens be glad and the earth rejoice!
Sing to the LORD a new song;
　　sing to the LORD, all you lands.
Sing to the LORD; bless his name;
　　announce his salvation, day after day.
Let the heavens be glad and the earth rejoice!
Let the heavens be glad and the earth rejoice
　　let the sea and what fills it resound;
　　let the plains be joyful and all that is in them!
Then shall all the trees of the forest exult before
　　　　the LORD.
Let the heavens be glad and the earth rejoice!
The LORD comes,
　　he comes to rule the earth.
He shall rule the world with justice
　　and the peoples with his constancy.
Let the heavens be glad and the earth rejoice!

Sunday, January 1
Solemnity of
Mary, the Holy Mother of God

For the yoke that burdened them, the pole on their shoulder, the rod of their taskmaster you have smashed, as on the day of Midian. . . . For a child is born to us, a son is given us; upon his shoulder dominion rests. They name him Wonder-Counselor, God-Hero, Father-Forever, Prince of Peace.
—Isaiah 9:3, 5

Isaiah sees a day when a great burden will be lifted off our shoulders as we walk in the light—but then he says something quite unexpected, something we have heard so many times or are so familiar with that we take it for granted but is actually totally shocking.

The incredible help we are going to receive is going to come from a child. It is a baby who will be born to help us to carry our burdens. The child is not any child but Wonder-Counselor, God-Hero, Father-Forever, Prince of Peace. In other words, the child will be the Son of God. Six hundred and fifty years before Jesus was born, the prophet Isaiah prophesied that God would send a child into the world to lead us to the light.

On this feast day celebrating the Virgin Mary's motherhood, thank God that he so loved the world he gave you his Son to show you the light and to carry your burdens. Pray for the grace to remember to invite Jesus to share your burdens throughout the new year.

Monday, January 2

For you were once in darkness, but now you are light in the Lord. Live as children of light, for light produces every kind of goodness and righteousness and truth. Try to learn what is pleasing to the Lord.

—Ephesians 5:8–10

Paul writes to the Ephesians that they were once in darkness. When they lived apart from Christ, they were in sin and darkness. Through Baptism, they are now in the light of the Lord. They are to walk in the light of the Lord, which is everything we know to be right and true and good. As children of the light, we look to please the Lord and to grow more and more to understand what pleases him.

....

Ask the Lord to show you what is good and right and the true things he wants you to do today. Pray for the grace to please him this day and throughout this new year.

Tuesday, January 3

Take no part in the unfruitful works of darkness; rather expose them. . . . Therefore, it says, "Awake, O sleeper, and arise from the dead, and Christ will give you light." Watch carefully then how you live, not as foolish persons but as wise, making the most of the opportunity, because the days are evil.
—Ephesians 5:11, 14–16

The world can tempt us toward works of darkness. Paul says to expose them rather than join them. When we turn to Jesus, he will give us the light we need to make wise decisions about how we spend our time and our days. The days or the times can tempt us toward evil and darkness. In every culture and every age there is thinking that is opposed to God's thinking. Every culture and age has some darkness. Jesus leads us to the light.

....

Pray for the grace to walk in wise ways this year. Ask Jesus to light your way and help you avoid the darkness and confusion of our current age.

Wednesday, January 4

Now this is the message we have heard from him and proclaim to you: God is light, and in him there is no darkness at all. If we say, "We have fellowship with him," while we continue to walk in darkness, we lie and do not act in truth. But if we walk in the light as he is in the light, then we have fellowship with one another, and the blood of his Son Jesus cleanses us from all sin.

—1 John 1:5–7

God is light. There is no darkness in him. To walk with God means to walk in the light of truth and to rid ourselves of every sin.

St. Thomas Aquinas prayed that God would remove the double darkness of sin and ignorance into which he and every human being is born. We are born with original sin and an orientation toward sin. We are born ignorant of the truth. We need the light of Christ to dispel both so we can live in fellowship and friendship with one another.

....

Thank your heavenly Father today that he has sent his Son into the world to drive away the double darkness of sin and ignorance. Pray for the grace to walk in fellowship with others today.

Thursday, January 5

The way we came to know love was that he laid down his life for us; so we ought to lay down our lives for our brothers. If someone who has worldly means sees a brother in need and refuses him compassion, how can the love of God remain in him? Children, let us love not in word or speech but in deed and truth.

—1 John 3:16–18

God lights our way by giving us an example in his Son, Jesus. We know the truth of God's love whenever we look at a crucifix: Jesus laid down his life for us. As we see the light of this truth, we are to lay down our lives for others. We are to offer compassion and support.

....

Take a moment to look at a crucifix. If you do not have one, close your eyes and picture Jesus on the Cross. See the love God has shown you. Invite the light of that truth into your heart. Then pray for the grace to have compassion today for three people, to love them in deed and in truth.

Friday, January 6

Arise! Shine, for your light has come, the glory of the Lord has dawned upon you. Though darkness covers the earth, and thick clouds, the peoples, upon you the Lord will dawn, and over you his glory will be seen. Nations shall walk by your light, kings by the radiance of your dawning.

—Isaiah 60:1–3

We are to rise up in God's splendor. Our light has come in the person of Jesus Christ. While there might be darkness in the world, the light of Christ shines in every single Christ follower. His glory is upon us so that the people around us will know the way to live. They will see our example of love and learn to walk by our light.

....

Thank God today that he calls you to be light in this dark work. Pray that others will see the light of Christ in you and learn to walk by your light.

Rev. Michael White and **Tom Corcoran** are coauthors of the bestselling Rebuilt Parish series, including the award-winning *Rebuilt, Tools for Rebuilding, Rebuilding Your Message, The Rebuilt Field Guide*, and *ChurchMoney*, as well as the bestselling Messages series for Advent and Lent. White serves as pastor and Corcoran as pastoral associate at Church of the Nativity in the Archdiocese of Baltimore. Together they lead the Rebuilt Parish Association. They are the hosts of the CatholicTV series *The Rebuilt Show*. White and Corcoran have spoken at conferences and parishes throughout the United States and Canada and at diocesan gatherings and conferences in Austria, Australia, Germany, Ireland, Poland, and Switzerland. They have been guests on EWTN, CatholicTV, Salt + Light Television, and numerous Catholic radio programs.

churchnativity.com
rebuiltparish.com
rebuiltparish.podbean.com
Facebook: churchnativity
Twitter: @churchnativity
Instagram: @churchnativity